MICHAEL "CLEATS" YAEGER

and

BRIAN "WAKEFIELD" DUNN

with the assistance of
SQI PR Director
Peter "Schultz" Cooper

and with illustrations by
Sarah "Watercolors Fresh Daily" Clementson

(a *folie à quatre*)

STUDIO SOLSTONE • *SEATTLE*

The various members of the "Wakefield" and
"Flegenheimer" families depicted herein are
whimsical creations. Any resemblance to any
actual persons, living or dead, is entirely
coincidental.

- The Authors -

SQUIM: The Untold Story

By Michael Yaeger and Brian E. Dunn
From an original idea by Michael Yaeger

Illustrated by Sarah Clementson

First Edition

ISBN: 0-931693-03-9

ACKNOWLEDGEMENTS

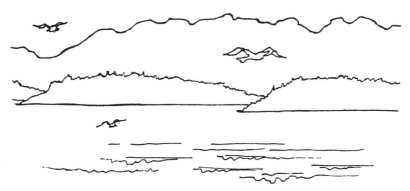

This book would not have been possible without the assistance of our talented and perceptive illustrator, Sarah ("Watercolors Fresh Daily") Clementson. Special thanks is also due the original "Master Thumper" himself, M. "Cleats" Yaeger, who graciously consented to fly his Lear jet up from Papeete for an extended series of interviews with the Squim Institute. Excerpts from the series (soon to be published *in toto* by SQI as *Dancin' in the Dark*) appear throughout this book.

- *SQI*

"For the preservation of the Little Ones, deep in the mud. . ."

Chapter 1

MONARCH OF THE MUDFLAT
The Untold Story of the Squim

This book, prepared by the Squim Institute (SQI), reveals a surprising Northwest secret: the present-day existence beneath Puget Sound mudflats of an actual "living fossil," the Original Squim (*Panope originalis*).

The book is arranged in three parts:

- **History and overview of the squim, the industry it created, and their present dilemma**
- **How you, personally, can help save both the squim and the industry from extinction**
- **Excerpts from** *Dancin' in the Dark*,[1] **an insider's look at the world of the squim**

Some of the questions this book will answer are: What is the cultural and economic importance of the squim? What is the *real* source of the finest "pigskin" leather? What do squim and Freud have in common? What has brought about the present danger to the squim?[2]

1. Soon to be published in 24 volumes by SQI.

2. If this slender volume doesn't answer all your questions, you may want to become a charter subscriber to *The Squim Encyclopedia*, a 30-volume work currently in progress. Write the Squim Institute for details.

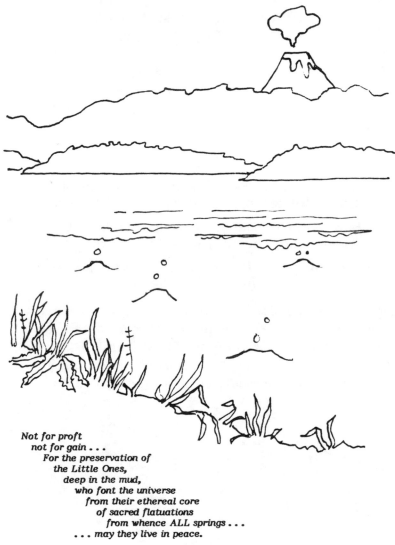

Not for proft
 not for gain . . .
   For the preservation of
    the Little Ones,
     deep in the mud,
      who font the universe
       from their ethereal core
        of sacred flatuations
         from whence ALL springs . . .
          . . . may they live in peace.

Morning Prayer at SQI
-from "Paean to the Squim"
Collected Verse
Dr. Mortimer H. Wakefield

Chapter 2
CHRONOLOGY

- PREHISTORIC -

circa 380,000,000 B.P.[1]

- First appearance of *Panope originalis* (the Original Squim) in the fossil record

circa 67,000,000 B.P.

- First near extinction of the Original Squim
- Squim colonies reach depths of 60 feet
- Extinction of *Torporsaurus ravenous*

- HISTORIC -

300 B.C.
- First recipe for baked squim with lemon (according to Cleats Yaeger)

1860
- Dr. Selig Heywood Wakefield, rediscoverer of the squim and founder of Wakefield Industries, born in London, England

1885
- M. "Cleats" Yaeger born in Portland, Oregon
- Selig H. Wakefield, with wife Bertha, arrives in Seattle via Boston

---

1. "Before Present," not "British Petroleum."

1886   • Birth of Mortimer H. Wakefield, son of Selig and Bertha

1888   • Birth of Victoria Wakefield, daughter of Selig and Bertha

1889   • The Great Seattle Fire
        • Disappearance of Bertha
        • Selig Wakefield, financially ruined by fire, moves to Port Townsend

1895   • First meeting between Selig Wakefield and Cleats Yaeger

1896   • Selig and Cleats capture their first squim
        • Selig discovers the commercial potential of the squim

1897   • The Alaska Gold Rush
        • First successful marketing of squimskin products as pigskin leather
        • First recorded appearance of the acronym "squim" in the New Orleans Picayune Times
        • Death of Cleats' parents in a tragic boating accident (bodies never recovered)

        • Selig attempts to adopt Cleats
        • Reconciliation between Selig and Cleats

1899   • The grim Squim War
        • Second near extinction of the Original Squim

1923   • Victoria "Schultzy" Flegenheimer (nee Wakefield) reconciles with her father after 34 years

1924	• Founding of Wakefield Industries as a partnership between Selig, Victoria, and her husband, Ruston "Schultz" Flegenheimer
1932	• Mortimer Wakefield returns from Paris after a brief incarceration in La Salpetriere (an unfortunate case of mistaken identity)
	• Cleats hired as Master Thumper at Wakefield Industries' main processing plant in Tacoma, Washington
1934	• Founding of the Squim Institute at Sequim, Washington (see Publisher's Note on the back cover)
1934	• Dr. Mortimer Wakefield appointed first director of the Squim Institute
	• Disappearance of the infamous "Palermo Pair" from the Museum of Commerce and Industry in Palermo

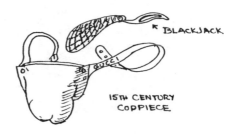

1940	• Peter "Schultz" Cooper, 10-year-old Rome war orphan, adopted by Victoria and Ruston

	• Birth of identical twins, Brian and Heywood Wakefield, sons of Mortimer Wakefield by Annette (Suzette?) St. Germain
1948	• Wakefield Industries' first "Annual Family Boat Outing"; Selig falls overboard and nearly drowns

1949   • Rediscovery of the "Palermo Pair" in West Berlin
   • Victoria Flegenheimer tragically drowns during Wakefield Industries' second "Annual Family Boat Outing" (body never recovered)

   • Ruston Flegenheimer nearly dies from arsenic poisoning
   • Peter "Schultz" Cooper returns to Palermo for "classical studies"

1950   • Mortimer Wakefield drowns during third "Annual Family Boat Outing" (body never recovered)

1958   • Selig Wakefield drowns during 10th "Annual Family Boat Outing" (body never recovered)

1970   • Heywood Wakefield goes to Paris to study mime

1980   • Cleats retires from Wakefield Industries just before 32nd "Annual Family Boat Outing"
   • Heywood returns to U.S. and establishes reputation as calendar artist

1985   • Wakefield Industries closed down by the EPA for failure to meet emissions standards
   • First closures of independent squim farms
   • Brian Wakefield-Dunn appointed new director of SQI
   • Peter "Schultz" Cooper appointed P.R. director at SQI

1985	• Heywood Wakefield disappears during "Annual Family Boat Outing" of the Arkansas Calendar Society
1986	• All squimmeries closed
	• SQI discovers that the cattle-prod management technique used by independent squimmeries has brought the Original Squim to the brink of extinction for the third time
	• Cleats finally willing to tell his story
	• Publication of *SQUIM: The Untold Story*
	• Preparations for the 38th "Annual Family Boat Outing," arranged by Peter "Schultz" Cooper

"For all what them little critters been through they shore 'nuff proved they is survivors. I'd say they rank right up there with the shark, rat, and cockroach. Betcha straight that given half a chance they'd go on survivin'..."

- *Dancin' in the Dark*

Chapter 3
BRIEF HISTORY OF THE SQUIM

As noted in the chronology, the Original Squim can be traced to a shadowy beginning in the lower Devonian period of the Paleozoic era, approximately 380 million years ago. The fossil record is sketchy until the middle Triassic, after which an abundance of fossilized remains clearly shows the Original Squim in its fully developed form.[1]

Some authorities[2] believe that the Original Squim was responsible for the extinction of the quaint "mud-flat dinosaur" (*Torporsaurus ravenous*) which, in turn, was responsible for the first near extinction of the squim. Proponents of this curious theory maintain that *Torporsaurus* became dependent on the defenseless squim for food, grew fat and lazy, and finally died of starvation when the squim colonies learned to defend themselves by burrowing to greater and greater depths.[3]

1. Expanded Squim Institute facilities, presently under construction, include a musuem and interpretive center.

2. Perhaps "authorities" is the wrong word. An examination of the literature on invertebrate paleontology reveals that those who have published monographs on the squim have (to be charitable) somewhat less than reassuring credentials.

3. For an interesting rebuttal of the hypothesis of squim-saurian symbiosis, see T. Rex's thoughtful and provocative *Dinosaur Diets: Fads and Fallacies*.

Until fairly recently, the scientific community assumed that the squim followed *Torporsaurus* into oblivion. Over the years, scattered reports of squimlike creatures were classified with similar "sightings" of the Loch Ness monster, the "sidehill gouger"[4] of British Columbia, and a variety of bizarre creatures reputedly lurking in the remote depths of the Amazon Basin and the African jungles.

The late 19th century rediscovery of the squim by Dr. Selig H. Wakefield, father of the squim industry, did little to change this situation[5] since the scientific community was never apprised of his findings.

---

4. Perhaps not as dubious a creature as the others cited. See e.g. L. M. Dill, "Behavioral Genetics of the Sidehill Gouger," *The Journal of Irreproducible Results,* New York: Workman Publishing, 1983.

5. Although Wakefield was, ironically, at least partly responsible for the second near extinction of the squim, as a result of the grim Squim War of 1899.

Even today, few people (outside the industry) are aware of the existence of these elusive creatures, which still make their homes deep beneath the surface of Puget Sound mudflats.

"My pet squim Gerty — thumped her up at a South End mudflat — got away from me once at a gas station in Olympia, Washington. Attendant thought she was a sponge filled with 30-weight nondetergent . . . almost squeezed her to death tryin' to wring 'er out, damn fool!"

- Dancin' in the Dark

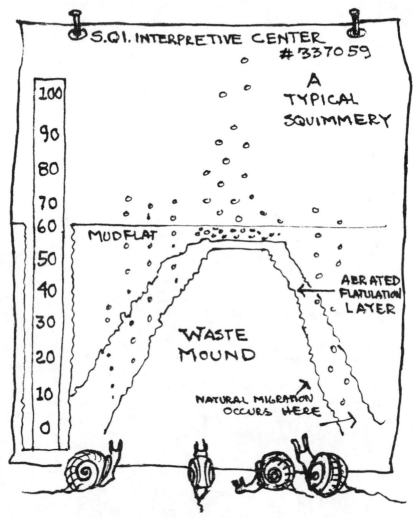

"Had a lot of fun with ol' Gerty . . . . There was an old coot livin' in a hotel in Port Townsend — drinkin' buddy of Selig's — who was sittin' down to write a letter on a crisp, clean white sheet of paper. Well, I plopped Gerty down right on top of that paper. Old Herman — that was his name — got so mad he throwed ol' Gerty in the trash can. She sure made an interestin' blot on that piece of paper. Old Herman let it dry, then carefully sealed it up and put it away. Crazy old guy. Herman . . . ? Herman . . . Rorschach? Yeah, that's it. Wonder what became of him?"

- Dancin' in the Dark

Chapter 4

BIOLOGICAL PROFILE

Environment. Squim live in colonies beneath
Puget Sound mudflats, where they thrive at depths of
up to 60 feet. Unlike any other known organism, direct
interaction with their own bodily wastes is necessary
to their survival. Gaseous decomposition products of
squim waste "aerate" a one-foot layer of the mudbed
just above the waste mound (see illustration). It is in
this aromatic region (the flatulation layer; see illustration) that squim larvae grow to adulthood relatively
free from molestation.[1]

▲

Development. During mating,[2] the female re-
leases a jellylike mass of 120,000 or more fertilized
eggs. Within 12 hours, these eggs develop into troco-
phore larvae that immediately began burrowing down-
wards toward the safety of the flatulation layer many
feet below.

1. The exception is self-molestation, an obsession of sexually awakening squim.
2. Assuming mating is heterosexual. See Chapter 5.

14

It is a perilous descent, and during the journey over 99 percent are eaten by various denizens of the mudflat. Those larvae which reach the flatulation layer are thenceforth safe from all known predators, and generally survive to adulthood without mishap. For the first year of their lives they spend the majority of their time eating and chasing bubbles (i.e., developing functional patterns of sexual behavior).

The Adult Squim. When a yearling leaves the safety of the flatulation layer to seek its fortune, it normally weighs about 10 pounds. The average weight for a 10-year-old adult is 40 pounds. This adult weight remains fairly constant for the next 20 years or so. A squim that survives beyond the age of 30 appears to crash through a kind of metabolic barrier. The catabolic processes normally associated with aging begin to reverse, and it once again begins to grow.[3]

3. It is at least theoretically possible for a 30-year-old squim to continue to survive and grow indefinitely. Thumpers have occasionally claimed to have spotted giant squim, and have reported estimated weights of 1,700 to 2,000 pounds. The extrapolated growth-age curve for a squim this large would indicate an age of 700 to 730 years. Unfortunately, no such specimen has ever been produced, so the existence of these ancient behemoths remains speculative. If they do exist, sightings would be extremely rare. Beyond a certain size a squim would be unattracted by the puny courtship-dance vibrations of an average-sized squim (see Chapter 5). It would probably take a properly trained 600-pound sumo wrestler to thump one up.

Natural Colony Expansion. During mating, the squims' energetic "dance of ecstasy" inevitably carries some partners beyond the perimeter of the waste mound. When they sink back, satiated, they naturally expand the colony (see illustration, page 12). [4]

"We got a real scientific handle on the size of a squimmery from a nutso type name of Leo. He used to appear from nowhere and stake out the dead center of a colony — directly over the waste mound — then hunker down and meddytate. Said it cleared his brains. Hell, I knew all along the seeds of solution were in those risin' bubbles. Well, Leo . . . Leo Trots? . . . Trotsky? Somethin' like that. Well, he just up and disappeared one day. Guess he found his solution for what was botherin' him."

- Dancin' in the Dark

---

4. Squim may appear sedentary, but we at SQI know that nature always finds a way.

"Squim absolutely fall in love with Wellingtons . . . wear 'em when you're out thumpin' you'd better be careful. When you're spread-eagled like that . . . Well, Gerty, my aforementioned pet squim, was attached to me for four months on account of I was too slow. Her bubbles melted one of my patented cleats . . . on my left Welly. I guess I got attached to her, too. Well, you could, you know . . ."

— *Dancin' in the Dark*

Chapter 5

REPRODUCTIVE BEHAVIOR

In addition to providing a safe home for maturing squim, the gas which bubbles up from the waste layer also tickles yearlings into a life-long sexual "high." Outwardly directed mating behavior occurs only once a month, however, during the full moon. At that time, all sexually mature squim attempt to attract mates by burrowing upwards to within six feet of the surface and rhythmically agitating themselves in a kind of "courtship dance."[1]

This dance is performed by both males and females, and (until the present crisis) either sex responded ecstatically. Since squim are perfectly happy copulating[2] with a member of either sex (or, for that matter, any moving object whose motion accurately simulates the courtship dance),[3] apart from making egg fertilization something of a crapshoot no real harm was done.[4]

---

1. Difficult to describe, but surprisingly catchy. In M. Cleats Yaeger's soon to be published *Dancin' in the Dark,* he says (Vol. 13, pg. 147), "I invented the 'thumper's movement,' that I'm sure Amos Milborn, the blues singer, turned into the Chicken Scratch dance that was popular in the early 50's. Same steps: 'Right, right, left, right, right,' stompin' all the time . . . ."

2. Perhaps a misnomer. Although mating squim do appear to "get it on," there is no actual joining of sex organs. Rather, each squim secretes a sticky substance that glues it to its partner, and brings the pair's respective sex organs into general proximity. Actual fertilization occurs outside the body.

3. The reader is cautioned to carefully read the section "What Can Go Wrong" in Chapter 9.

4. In spite of "thumper tales" about brawny bull squim inadvertently drowning young females in torrents of squim sperm. SQI, however, *has* authenticated numerous reports of generously endowed females suffocating young males beneath voluminous masses of eggs.

"One time at a bar in Port Townsend I got talkin' with this writer-inventor sort. O.K., maybe I was drinkin' some and perhaps had a loose tongue, but this guy started tellin' me how he figured thumpin' could be mechanized real easy. The fool was tryin' to mechanicalize me right out of my profession! What was his name? Frances? Frank? Franky Herbert? Somethin' like that. Hard to remember . . . was way back in the early 50's."

- *Dancin' in the Dark*

Chapter 6

BIRTH OF WAKEFIELD INDUSTRIES
Dr. Selig H. Wakefield: Man of Destiny

In 1885 Dr. Selig H. Wakefield, the visionary Boston surgeon, moved his thriving medical practice to Seattle. Shortly thereafter, he lost both his practice and his young wife in the Great Seattle Fire of 1889. These events, which would have crushed a lesser man, served only to spur him onward towards an even brighter future. After entrusting his two infant children to the care of their faithful nanny (who whisked them safely back to Cambridge), the intrepid doctor, harkening to the clarion call of destiny, forged onward to Port Townsend and his destiny—discovering the squim.

Though the good people of Port Townsend did not know their mudflats were rich with squim colonies, Dr. Wakefield was quick to discover their existence and realize their commercial potential. After months of exhaustive research and development he created one of the technological marvels of the late 19th century: a processing machine that converted "green" squimskin into a tough and durable pigskin-like material.

Wakefield's machine accounted in large part for Seattle's edge among Pacific Coast ports as an outfitter for gold seekers bound for the Klondike. He supplied gold seekers with supremely functional pack saddles, harness straps, boots, and belts of incredibly durable "pigskin" leather, not to mention many tons of Alaska Husky Feed.®

Wakefield's finished goods were only part of his operation, however. The finished "pigskin" was also supplied to other artisans, many of whose remarkable creations are still in use today. Examples include the couch on which Sigmund Freud conducted his first analysis, several dubious-looking "Egyptian mummies" in Chicago's Field Museum, and the elevator hoist cables in Seattle's Smith Tower and Harrad's of London. Less well-known (and less authenticated) examples include the suspenders John Wayne wore in his Academy Award-winning film, "True Grit," and the ceremonial lederhosen worn by Ernst Roehm's Brownshirts in pre-Nazi Germany.

The most bizarre examples, though, are undoubtedly the curious forgeries known as the "Palermo Pair." Long on display at Palermo's Museum of Commerce and Industry, the handsomely tooled blackjack and codpiece, which appear to be of late 15th century Italian[1] design, disappeared from the museum in 1934. Their whereabouts remained a mystery until 1949, when they were recovered from the rubble of a bombed-out West Berlin beer garden. At least one "authority"[2] has argued that they were briefly in the hands of the S.S., who attempted to use them as foci for concentrating and directing "occult energies" against the Allies.[3]

1. Reputed to be the work of Leonardo Da Vinci. The blackjack bears a striking resemblance to one of his *Notebooks* sketches.

2. I. Jones, 211.

3. There is strong evidence that the codpiece was once possessed by England's self-styled "black magician," A. Crowley.

If Wakefield was the Michelangelo of the squim, then his daughter, Victoria, was its Lee Iacocca. In 1923, after reconciling with her estranged father, Victoria assumed control of the business and moved it to its present location in the north end of Tacoma.[4]

It was her managerial acumen, combined with the financial backing her husband Ruston was able to secure, that turned Wakefield's visionary dream of a squim industrial empire into a reality. Wakefield Industries was born . . .

Between 1923 and 1985, the company has established itself as the number one supplier of "genuine simulated leather," distributed throughout the world to be fashioned into: Tanzanian Land Rover steering wheel covers; Kenyan "elephant's foot" umbrella stands; Swiss watch bands; Soviet cosmonaut helmets; Argentine bolos; Italian shoes; Japanese camera cases, watch fobs, etc.; Anglo-Indian officers' riding crops; U.S. "bedroom accessories"; Canadian Sam Browne belts; Australian boomerang holders, etc., etc., ad infinitum.[5]

Alas, this golden age may now be drawing to a close.

4. At Ruston's suggestion, to minimize distribution difficulties.

5. Our proudest and most patriotic moment came during World War II, when we made sure the Allies were supplied with Grade A materials, while relegating Grade B and lower to the Axis powers (whenever possible).

"Bein' six-foot-siz and 280 pounds helped a lot at my Master Thumpin' position. I could thump up a squim faster'n any other thumper. My secret was in how I created counter-rhythms by snappin' my suspenders — kind of a counterbeat to my cleats. There was a feller with a tape recorder one day, name of Dave . . . Dave Brubeck? I heard this jazz tune once, think they called it "Take Five." I always wondered . . . hmmm . . . naw, must've been a coincidence."

- Dancin' in the Dark

Chapter 7
DAWN OF A NEW TOMORROW

A Bitter Pill. In 1985 Wakefield Industries' Tacoma plant was closed down due to the smokestack emission of unacceptably high levels of arsenic (a natural byproduct of squim processing). This created a ripple effect throughout the squim industry. Suddenly, independent squim farmers (upon whom Wakefield Industries had become increasingly dependent for raw materials) had no market for their harvest, and squimmeries began closing their doors, abandoning their colonies to fate.

In early 1986 the Squim Institute began conducting feasibility studies for on-site processing at the abandoned squimmeries. Almost immediately, however, SQI researchers uncovered a problem far graver than economic loss: one which heavily impacts all squim colonies and poses a serious threat to the very survival of the species.

The Seeds of Disaster. This problem stems from an abhorrent squim-farm management technique known as "cattle-prod" management. The technique (not used at Wakefield Industries' own plant until after 1980) appears to have been standard practice at all independent squimmeries, where it seems profits were considered more important than responsible husbandry.

Briefly, "cattleprod" management involved surrounding each colony with electrified probes inserted deep into the mud. This increased population density and harvest yields by interfering with the colony's natural expansion mechanism (see "Natural Colony Expansion" in Chapter 4). Even so, as long as the colonies were heavily harvested no adverse effect was apparent.

Unfortunately, the cessation of harvesting activities following the closure of the squim farms resulted in a population explosion. Severe overcrowding disrupted normal mating behavior, and courtship dancing began to resemble an 18th century minuet more than the energetic 1950's sockhop gyrations of healthy squim.

This process is now so far advanced the languid dancing of the squim no longer attracts partners of either sex, and *no* mating, heterosexual or otherwise, is now occurring.

A Tangled Web. Though renewed harvesting would reduce population density to safe levels, it will not solve the problem. The threat to species survival is due to a combination of two factors: (1) Since the behavioral change is irreversible, sexually mature squim will continue to be incapable of mating with each other, even after normal population density is restored; (2) The delay between the onset of the problem and its discovery means that all squim larvae have since matured, and therefore *all* squim are by now sexually dysfunctional. Using wild squim as sex therapists would solve the problem, but unfortunately is not an option: there are no wild squim.[1] They were long ago thumped up and captured by greedy squim farmers who added them to their squimmeries to increase production.

The Glimmer of Hope. Fortunately, there is a solution. The squim can be saved and the colonies can be restored—but only with your help.

We at SQI recognize that our industry is at least partly to blame for this unfortunate situation. Like the squim itself, we were rather "spineless," and did not adequately supervise our suppliers. But we have learned from our mistakes, resolved not to repeat them, and are ready to do our part in making amends.

---

1. At least none known to be sexually active. Just in case a slumbering giant is located in some remote mudflat, however, we have contacted all sumo wrestling schools in Tokyo on the off-chance an emerging 600-pounder may need some extra lunch money and be interested in learning how to thump.

In this time of crisis, we have developed two exciting and innovative programs that can ensure the survival of the squim. To implement them, however, we need *your* cooperation and involvement. Only by working together can we save the squim and restore it to its rightful throne as Monarch of the Mudflat.

"Hell, once with Gerty . . . . Well, a squim'll mate with anything,
let me tell you. A group of those Barnum and Bailey circus types
travellin' through camped right near the mudflat. At midnight
durin' the full moon period, to everyone's surprise, the flats had
one of the largest squim colonies ever discovered. Well, the ele-
phants panicked, buckin' and trompin' with their shackled feet,
which in turn elevated the squim's ecstasy even higher. Well,
everybody and everything got a little piece of the action that night.
Heard Buffalo Bill was the feature show of that circus. Hmmm
. . . ."

- *Dancin' in the Dark*

Chapter 8

HELP SAVE THE SQUIM!
Appeal to the Reader

Now that the story of the squim is at last being told, the vital contribution the species has made to our modern world can be appreciated. In fact, it is plain that the squim ranks with the chicken and the cow as one of "God's pantheon of helpers of Man."[1] Yet today, and for the third time in the history of the species, the extinction of the squim is imminent.

How tragic it would be if the squim, which survived both the greed of the mudflat dinosaur and the ravages of the grim Squim War, should succumb to the lamentable short-sightedness of profit-hungry squim farmers. And it doesn't have to. Though the present crisis is the severest trial the species has ever faced, a glimmer of hope remains—with you. You, personally, can help save the squim from extinction, and—for once—know that your individual efforts *do* make a real difference.

How? By participating in either (or better, both) of the following SQI programs.

#1   MUDFLAT RESEEDING PROGRAM
"Milk a Squim for Uncle Mort"

#2   POPULATION REDUCTION PROGRAM
"Invite a Squim to Dinner"

The following three chapters detail the prerequisites for participating in program number one.

---

1. From "Paean to the Squim," page 137, *Collected Verse,* Dr. Mortimer H. Wakefield.

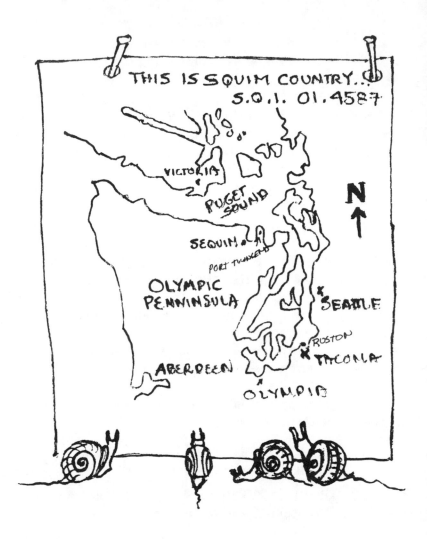

"I thumped all over the Sound. Know every squimmery. Even thumped off sound, explorin' for the company in Chesapeake Bay, Beverly Hills estuary, the Potomac, Hong Kong harbor, and Hobart. Never, never found another Original Squim squimmery. Yeah, lotsa cheap halfbreeds out there in the boondocks, but Big Time is here. So, as President Reagan says, we just gotta keep on thumpin'...."

- Dancin' in the Dark

Chapter 9

OBTAIN YOUR SQUIM

Available Options: (1) Purchase a black-market original from a professional thumper for $200 to $250; (2) Attempt to locate and capture a wild squim; or (3) capture your squim in an abandoned squimmery. The first option is definitely not recommended. Unemployed thumpers foist off everything from geoducks to moon snails on gullible buyers, and it is difficult to obtain the genuine article at any price. Since wild squim are so rare, the second option is also not recommended. If you could locate one, however, it would be an exhilarating adventure, requiring either imploring calls to Japan or a whole crew of professional thumpers to thump it up, a choreographer to keep them in synch, a crane to lift the beast, a two-ton flatbed to haul it. (In either case you'd need an olympic-size pool to house it.) Therefore, this chapter explains how to capture a squim in an abandoned squimmery.[1]

Recommended Equipment. As is true for any great hunt, you must first be properly clothed and have the necessary equipment. Dress warmly and take along a sturdy spade, a coal shovel, a thick army blanket, and a friend in good condition who weighs not less than 260 pounds. To maximize your chances of success, SQI recommends leaving your friend at home and hiring a skilled professional thumper. He will not only be trained in squim-harvesting techniques, but will also have the necessary percentage of body fat.

---

1. Make sure you've properly prepared a home habitat before actually capturing your squim (see Chapter 10).

"As a freelancer for the company I met a lot of their Catchers. All "Eyetalians" for some reason. Didn't have no weight, but boy were they quick at shovelin' bull squim! Lingered longer over the females, I noticed. Like that movie star, Marcello Mastroiani, they had a knack for tellin' the difference — somethin' I never could do."

                                              - Dancin' in the Dark

After you've assembled the necessary equipment, you need to know where to look. A map[2] showing the location of abandoned squimmeries is necessary but insufficient. To pinpoint the location of your quarry, you must first become acquainted with the habits of the species (as outlined in Chapters 4 and 5).

Digging Up Your Squim: After you've spotted the telltale bubbles and unforgettable fragrance of a squim (strangely reminiscent of Chanel No. 5), have your fat friend (or professional thumper) start bouncing,[3] spread-eagled, over the exact location where the bubbles are rising. Once he starts bouncing, he must be careful to maintain the proper rhythm.[4] Meanwhile, you must begin digging furiously in the mud between his legs. Don't worry about having to dig the whole six feet; your sex-starved squim will be as eager to reach you as you are to reach it. At the same time you are digging down, it will be rapidly tunneling upwards to meet (it thinks) its mate. Rendezvous generally takes place at a depth of about three feet.

As you dig, you must constantly monitor the frequency with which the rising bubbles burst. When the rate reaches 10 to 12 per minute, you will have almost reached the squim. At this point count to 100, then stop digging. Pick up the coal shovel and wait for the squim to emerge.[5]

2. A three-color map showing the locations of abandoned squimmeries, printed on oilskin and complete with an attractive mudproof carrying case, is available from the Squim Institute for just $9.95.

3. *Fat,* not musclebound. A certain amount of "jiggling" is a necessary component of the vibration being induced; if absent, the squim will not be agitated into the necessary mating frenzy.

4. A Sony Walkman or its equivalent is a useful accessory. Selections that can help your thumper maintain the proper rhythm include Ravel's "Bolero," certain passages of Stravinsky's "Rite of Spring," and anything by John Philip Sousa or Jerry Lee Lewis.

5. When you see what appears to be a giant pulsating inkblot explode upward out of the mud, that will probably be it.

"I hold the thumper's endurance record. Seven and a half hours, same rhythm. We hauled out the biggest squim on record on that thump — 650 pounds. Record still stands. Took eight men. One of 'em was named James . . . James Mason, guy that invented the Mason jar.

- **Dancin' in the Dark**

What Can Go Wrong. Remember: not having mated in approximately two years, the squim will be sexually hyperactive. Be fast as you scoop it up. If you miss, and it attaches itself to your thumper's leg, you'll have a real battle on your hands. A squim in a mating frenzy will not let go until it expends itself completely, a process that can take as long as five hours.

If it is a bull squim, the sperm produce a stinging sensation rather like a nettle. This isn't dangerous unless the skin is broken and it enters the body.[6] If it is female, the egg mass planted on your thumper's leg will adhere so tightly it cannot be removed without considerable loss of skin. The biological "glue" responsible for this distressing phenomenon gradually deteriorates over a period of about four months, after which the egg mass will slough off of its own accord.[7]

Usually, though, all goes well. When the squim emerges, your thumper deftly leaps aside and you simply scoop it up with the coal shovel, wrap it in the wet army blanket, and rush it to its new home.[8]

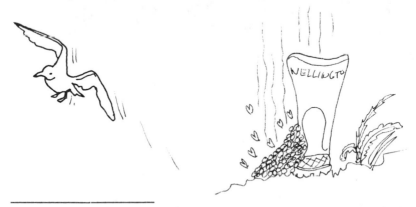

---

6. If it enters the bloodstream it can cause a distressing malady characterized by a craving for raw garden slugs and an urge to attend mud-wrestling matches.

7. The only known solvent for this "glue" is squim sperm, so the only other way to remove the egg mass is by soliciting the amorous advances of a male squim during a subsequent full moon.

8. Easy does it! Remember, in spite of its robust appearance a squim is an invertebrate and has no spine. Don't treat it like a football.

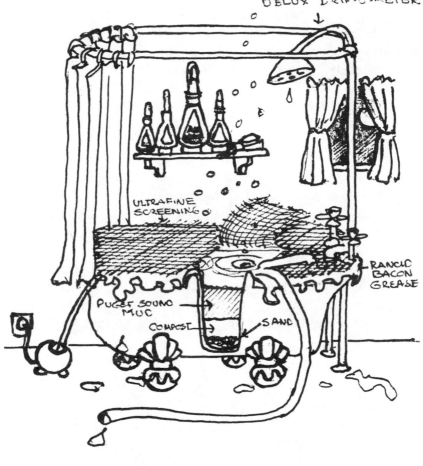

DELUX DRIP-O-METER

ULTRAFINE SCREENING

RANCID BACON GREASE

PUGET SOUND MUC

COMPOST

SAND

"My pet squim, Gerty, lived in my bathtub for seven years. Hell,
I only got one bathroom, but she wasn't in my way nohow . . . ."

- *Dancin' in the Dark*

Chapter 11

GIVE IT A HOME

Building Your Squim Habitat: You must duplicate your squim's natural habitat[1] as closely as possible. Follow this seven-step procedure to be sure of success:[2]

(1) Your first requirement is for a large tank or vat. You already have this in the form of your bathtub, which has the necessary water supply, drainage, etc.

(2) Prepare your bathtub by placing a fine screen[3] over the drain and a hose (long enough to reach to the other end of the tub) over the spigot.

(3) Spread two inches of gritty sand in the bottom of the tub.[4]

(4) Lay a three inch thick bed of specially formulated compost[5] over the sand. You will never have to change the compost; your squim's bodily wastes will quickly take over that function.

> *"There was a time I was really into thumpin', experimentin' at different hours and days other'n full moon. Hell, I moved into a mudflat with Gerty when she attached herself to me . . . in the early 30's that was. Know how you get to know your dog, like? Well, that was like me and Gerty the first time I saw her eyes. They was under hundreds of wrinklelike droops. She shore was a shy cuss . . . but oh so soulful! Kinda like Paul Neuman."*
>
> **— Dancin' in the Dark**

1. Better yet, consider moving your own household onto your squim's mudflat. *The Compleat Mudsteader: Use Ooze to Build Your Dream House,* complete with working drawings, is available from the Squim Institute for just $24.95.
2. Save time and frustration by ordering our "Complete Squim Habitat Kit," which includes everything you need to convert your bathtub into the ideal squim habitat. Only $199.95 from the Squim Institute.
3. Any galvanized screen having 16 squares to the inch is acceptable.
4. Prime "Spanish Riviera" sand is available from the Squim Institute for just $19.95 per 50-pound bag.
5. Custom-formulated, scientifically balanced Squimpost® may be obtained from the Squim Institute for just $9.95 per 25-pound bag.

(5) Fill the remainder of the tub with genuine Puget Sound mud, purchased from a reputable mud dealer and free of heavy-metal pollution.[6]

(6) Smear the rim of the tub with rancid bacon grease,[7] to which squim have a strong aversion.[8]

(7) Let your squim habitat rest for two weeks. During this time check to make sure that you have rigged the hose properly and that a constant drip[9] of water moistens the mud at regular intervals (see illustration). After about 10 days large bubbles will begin to form on the surface of the mud, indicating that the habitat is ready for occupancy.[10]

---

6. Laboratory analysis is available through the Squim Institute. Just send us a hermetically sealed 36-ounce jar of mud, along with your check or money order for $24.95.

7. Acceptable substitutes include: (1) a thick paste made of equal parts freeze-dried eggs and rancid mayonnaise, (2) a thick coat of creosote, or (3) narrow strips torn from unwashed sweatsocks and glued to the tub's rim with epoxy cement.

8. During the full moon your squim will feel the urge to investigate any unusual vibrations. This simple precaution will keep your squim from leaving its own bed and possibly ending up in yours.

9. Rate should be between 8 and 10 cc's per hour. Our Deluxe Drip-O-Meter,® with state-of-the-art microchip technology, is available for just $59.95. In addition to precisely metering water flow, the Deluxe Drip-O-Meter® also regulates the impact force of the water to assure proper volume level and musical pitch: important considerations for your squim's rapid psychological adjustment to its new home.

10. It would be wise to have it checked by one of our experts before installing your squim. Write for additional information.

Installing Your Squim: For about six hours after capture, your squim will remain in an intense sexual high. When it is plunked down into your bathtub it will neither know nor care where it is. When this high fades to a normal level of generalized sexual excitement, your squim will begin exploring and settling into its new abode.

Adjustment Period. There is a one-year period of adjustment during which your squim should be monitored at least four times a day to ensure it remains in good health and is adapting satisfactorily. If it survives this adjustment period you can expect to have it for some time to come[11] (assuming you carefully follow Chapter 11's feeding recommendations).

A Word of Caution: When the moon is full be careful not to agitate your squim, and be especially careful not to dance or jump up and down within 20 feet of its habitat. In fact, the Squim Institute recommends entirely avoiding your bathroom when the moon is full.

11. In fact, recent research suggests that squim kept in home habitats are likely to break through the 30-year metabolic barrier (see Chapter 4, footnote 3). It is therefore wise to make some provision for your squim in your will in the event it survives you. Appropriate will forms, with complete instructions, are available from the Squim Institute for just $9.95.

"Gerty was the most finicky-eatin' squim I ever knowed. She swore off banana one day. Then, Whup! she went on a total hunger strike till I introduced her to guacamole. Got her back on diet by carefully mincin' some slug and snails in with the guoc. Trouble was, she got hooked on avocado. Changed her smell, sort of. One of the reasons we had a partin' of the ways . . . ."

- *Dancin' in the Dark*

Chapter 11
NOW . . . FEED IT

A squim will eat just about anything it encounters in its natural habitat. In your bathtub, however, not just anything comes along. You will have to try to duplicate your squim's natural dietary intake as closely as possible.

Basic Squim Nutrition. In general, snails and slugs are excellent staples for every other day. For some reason wild mushrooms (preferably boletes and chanterelles) are necessary for the proper nutrition of a captive squim. They must be freshly gathered (no more than two days old) and free of infestation by insects or other vermin. You will also need to feed three ounces of sturgeon caviar per week. Goat's milk is also important, as are bananas (peeled and chopped).

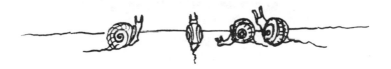

The Squim Diet. The following scientifically balanced diet will provide 100 percent of an adult squim's nutritional requirements for one week. Serve half portions to a yearling. After preparation, all foodstuffs should be injected[1] at least one foot deep into the mud.

---

1. For best results, use an OOSI® (Optimum Organic Sludge Injector), available from the Squim Institute for just $39.95.

Monday/Wednesday/Friday

Breakfast 2   4-inch slugs (live)
             4   ounces wild mushrooms
             2   bananas (peeled and chopped)

Lunch   1   4-inch slug
             4   ounces wild mushrooms
             1   medium apple[2] (minced)

Dinner   6   4-inch slugs (mashed and blended with
                 one quart fresh goat's milk[3]
             3   bananas (peeled and chopped)

Tuesday/Thursday/Saturday

Breakfast 2   3-inch snails (shelled)[4]
             4   ounces wild mushrooms
             2   bananas (peeled and chopped)

Lunch   1   3-inch snail (shelled)
             4   ounces wild mushrooms
             1   bunch of radishes (minced)[5]

Dinner   6   4-inch snails (shelled), mashed,
                 and blended with one quart
                 goat's milk
             3   bananas (peeled and chopped)

Menu for Sunday breakfast and lunch is the same as for Monday, Wednesday, and Friday, but add three ounces of caviar for Sunday dinner.

---

2. Preferably a Granny Smith or Winesap.

3. Since goat's milk must be *absolutely fresh* and at goat-temperature, it is advisable to have your own goat. A list of recommended goat breeders in your area is available from the Squim Institute for just $1.95.

4. Common garden snails are acceptable, though imported escargot is strongly recommended. Recent research suggests that domesticated squim fed garden snails rather than escargot tend to become surly and withdrawn.

5. White radishes are preferred. The skin of a red radish is toxic to a squim, so if you must use them be sure to peel them carefully.

Substitutions: Eels may be used instead of slugs and snails. Canned truffles are an accpetable substitute for wild mushrooms. Squash can take the place of bananas. Half and Half may be used instead of goat's milk. If caviar is a problem, try beluga instead of sturgeon. [1]

General Advice: Though surprisingly adaptable creatures, squim are violently intolerant and unforgiving of second-rate food and indifferent preparation. It is not unknown for a disgruntled squim to go on a hunger strike. Keep your squim fat and sassy by preparing its food with care and strictly adhering to the dietary regime outlined above.

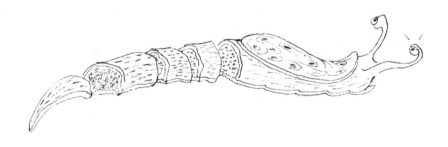

1. Cleats says, "If your squim don't take to caviar, try my 'Seattle Chili White' recipe. Good for what ails your squim and for what ails you. Don't be afraid to improvise, like that Charlie Parker guy. Knew him once .... But here's the recipe. Just fry up half a pound of bacon till crisp, cool your flame, and add a whole bulb of chopped garlic and a couple of pours of tamari. Let it simmer a bit, then drain it and set it aside. Chop up fine two fresh, medium-size geoducks. Fry 'em in bacon fat till they're crisp and set 'em aside. Boil up a pound of lima beans, with lots of white peper and hot green peppers. When they're done, puree half of 'em, and set the puree aside. Mix together your bacon, geoduck, and puree, then add your beans. Mix in some raw choped carrots, onions, and walnuts before servin' it up. Make sure you serve it pipin' hot! Feeds six to eight hungry thumpers."

BASIC PROCEDURE

For "Mudflat Reseeding Program," showing equipment contained in SQI's $199.95 Basic Starter Set (write us for details).

1.   One deluxe, inflatable "Surrogate Squim"
2.   One industrial strength vibrator attachment
3.   One deluxe remote control unit for vibrator
4.   One carton of 12 gamete bag attachments
5.   One carton of 12 blue ice packets
6.   12 styrofoam shipping cartons

Chapter 12

SQI'S "SAVE THE SQUIM" PROGRAMS

The "Milk a Squim for Uncle Mort"[1] program (which requires some equipment investment) provides a means whereby concerned citizens, in the comfort and privacy of their homes, can simulate the mating dance of a healthy squim and induce a captive squim to "donate" much-needed sperm or eggs. The "Invite a Squim to Dinner" program (which requires no special equipment) will help by simultaneously reducing the bloated squim population in preparation for mudflat reseeding.

1. **Mudflat Reseeding Program** ("Milk a Squim for Uncle Mort"). To participate, you must first obtain the necessary equipment (see illustration).

The procedure itself is simple. On the night of the full moon, fill the Surrogate Squim ("SS") with warm jello, attach a gamete bag, and place it on the surface of your tub. Then leave the room and switch on the vibrator. Your sex-starved squim will waste no time in rising to the occasion and depositing a load of sperm or eggs in the gamete bag. After waiting a prudent interval (four or five hours), retrieve the SS, remove and seal the gamete bag, place it in a shipping container (with a packet of "blue ice"), and ship it to the Squim Institute.

Eggs and sperm received from participants will be combined at SQI's laboratories, and the resulting larvae will be used for reseeding the squimmeries.

---

1. As Dr. Mortimer H. Wakefield was affectionately known by his loyal staff (Colette St. Germain and her talented daughters, Suzette and Annette).

"You know those Everett commie riots back when? Well, it warn't the commies that ticked off the crowd, it was on account of some jackass tryin' to bake a squim but not havin' enough sense to follow the recipe. Now pay attention, folks . . . you don't want to have any unnecessary casualties to deal with . . . ."

— Dancin' in the Dark

2. **Population Reduction Program** ("Invite a Squim to Dinner"). To participate, simply thump up a squim at an abandoned squimmery. A wide variety of unforgettable squim dishes, including casseroles, beverages, and desserts may be found in M. "Cleats" Yaeger's *A Gourmand's Guide to the Squim,* available from the Squim Institute for just $14.95. Cleats' favorite recipe is reproduced here.

SQUIM BULLING

INGREDIENTS

1 squim (30 pounder, filleted)	1 gal. wine vinegar
1 quart unsulfered molasses	1 bull kelp (35-foot)

PREPARATION

1. Dive down into kelp bed and snip off (at the basal holdfast) a bull kelp about 35 feet long. Section stem into two-foot lengths, discarding fronds.

2. Let stem sections dry in bright sunlight for two weeks. If you don't live in the banana belt, you may have to use your oven instead (slowly dry at 110° for 20 hours). Coarsely grate when thoroughly dry.

3. Marinate grated kelp in vinegar-molasses marinade. Do not disturb for two weeks.

4. Add squim fillets and marinate two more weeks.

5. Place fillets on several sections of aluminum foil, turning up edges to form shallow pans. Drizzle with remaining marinade. Cover and seal with foil.

6. Bake 24 hours in fire pit lined with smooth beach stones.

7. While tending the squim and keeping watch, wear a Navy-issue Type-20 detox gas mask.[1]

8. Serve with butter lettuce, radish, and garlic salad. Baby peas and baked Finn potatoes make excellent accompaniments. For wine, a hearty French Burgundy or a thick, country-style Peruvian Red is suggested.

---

1. Available from the Squim Institute for just $69.95.

THE SQUIM INSTITUTE
P.O. BOX 4304

PIONEER SQUARE
SEATTLE, WA 98104

PLEDGE

—§—

*Now that you're acquainted
with SQI's programs, it's time
to make a commitment*

Take up the SQI banner and march
towards the mudflats and the
dawn of a new day for the squim
by taking one (or both) of the following pledges:

Pledge #1

I pledge to participate in SQI's
"Milk a Squim for Uncle Mort"
by seducing (insert number) ____
squim. In turn, SQI pledges to
give me a 10% discount on all
necessary equipment.

Pledge #2

I pledge to participate in SQI's
"Invite a Squim to Dinner" program by eating (insert number;
minimum two) ____ squim per
week. In turn SQI pledges to give
me a 10% discount on the
cookbook and gas mask.

_____
SIGNATURE

_____
SQI APPROVAL

"Once outside Bremerton, Washington, I come across a foreigner and his son tryin' to fix a flat on their Bugatti. The tire was tore up so bad it was useless, but I happened to have along a bucket of squim I'd thumped up the previous night. So I helped 'em out by tying a squim in a knot, and together we managed to ooze the sucker around the rim. 'Fore you knowed it, they was on the road again. Thank God I had three gas masks with me or we'da all gagged dead from the effort. Name was . . . Chuck? Charles? Charles Dunlop? Somethin' like that . . . ."

- Dancin' in the Dark

Chapter 13

"DANCIN' IN THE DARK"
An Excerpt

The following extended excerpt from SQI's series of interviews with the remarkably well-preserved Mr. M. "Cleats" Yaeger (who just celebrated his 101st birthday) is included out of reverence for the memory of Dr. Selig H. Wakefield. Although Mr. Yaeger was, and remains, close to the family, the reader is cautioned that some of his recollections are either gross exaggerations or outright fabrications.

SQI: How did you and Dr. Wakefield meet?

Cleats: *When I was 10 I used to spend a lot of time pokin' about the mudflats. Bein' 200 pounds I had a tendency to kinda sink out of sight if I stood in one place too long, and Selig sometimes had to pull me outta the muck . . . .*

SQI: Did you spend a lot of time together?

Cleats: *Yeah. 'Twas right after the big Seattle Fire of '89 . . . he sort of wandered up to Port Townsend in a daze, right smack dab into the heart of squim country . . . 'cept no one knew, then. Townfolks called the mudbanks "P.U." 'cause the smell was so bad. He built hisself a shack on the edge of the mudflats, and was survivin' on geoducks and booze while he tried to regroup his life. Still had his machine, or at least what was left of it . . . and like that Gandhi feller with his spinnin' wheel, he'd grind away at imaginary flesh throughout the night whenever he got melancholy . . .*

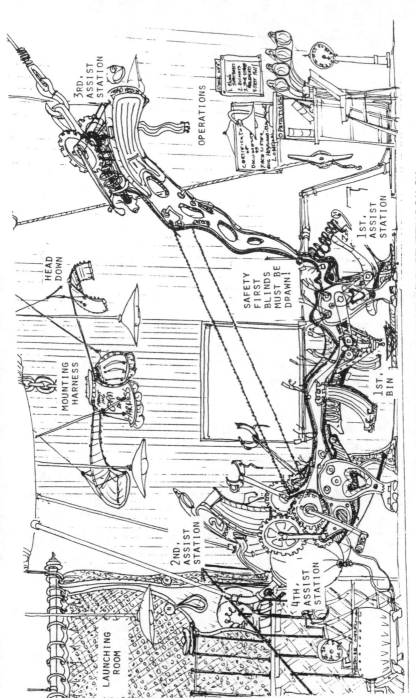

WELCOME TO DR. SELIG H. WAKEFIELD'S FACELIFTING SALON
(and excess poundage remover)

BOSTON, MASSACHUSETTS - founded in 1884 - FREE ESTIMATES

SQI: What else do you recall about his machine?

Cleats: *That was some contraption, all right . . . needed four strappin' young men to run that old beasty. Whatever the trouble was that made him leave Boston with it and his troupe of "assistants," he ended up in Seatty [ed. "Seattle"]. Here, check out this old drawing. That was where he opened his salon for faceliftin' society matrons' faces. Trouble was, unlike Boston, there warn't no society matrons in Seattle. Come to think of it, warn't many "ladies" for that matter, and his business went from bad to worse. 'Fore long he was on the skids . . . had to let his assistants go, and then the fire took everything he had, 'cept'n the guts of his machine. There was a solid core of mean face stretchers and carbon-steel flesh pounders underneath all that frilly lace and pink padding, where his and his fellers' fingers 'n tools stuck through during an operation. That's what survived the fire . . . .*

SQI: Were you with him when he first discovered a squim?

Cleats: *I shore was. After my folks died, he took me in. Tried to give me a classical education, but it never come to much 'cause of his drinking. Anyway, I remember one night at full moon — full moons used to get him dancin' away — well, we was hungry so we went out to the flats to get us a geoduck. He'd had a snootfull, and was a-carryin' on some, when one popped up clean out of the mud right next to us, just like it was curious to see what was goin' on. We'd never seen one do such a thing before, but Selig was quick as a whip even when he was three sheets to the wind, and he nabbed the critter afore it knew what'd hit it, and we plunked it into the bucket. It was overcast and drizzlin', and too dark to see much, so we didn't get a good look at it until we got back to the shack. That's when we realized we'd made some kind of mistake. At the time, we thought it was just about the godawfulest-lookin' thing we'd ever seen. Scared hell out of the both of us, I don't mind tellin' you . . . looked like the clotted throwaways out of a well-used spittoon. Well, Selig, he chucked the thing out the window in disgust, and unbeknownst to us, it landed in his machine out on the porch . . . .*

SQI: Then how was it that. . . .

Cleats: *Don't interrupt, boy . . . I ain't through tellin' it yet! Later on that night he got into one of his grindin' moods, went out on the porch, and next thing you know . . . Whoops! Out pops the finest piece of leather you ever laid eyes on. Looked just like prime pigskin.*

SQI: So that's when he realized he was on to something?

Cleats: *Not rightaways. Next mornin' he had a whale of a hangover and couldn't rightly remember what had happened the night before. But something kept naggin' at him, and he kept a-worryin' and a-frettin' about it all mornin' long. I was too young to understand the significance of the situation, but I could see that somethin' powerful important was botherin' him. Anyway, I mentioned the horrible critter he'd chucked out the night before, and it was just like a light bulb'd gone on over his head. He went into a regular thinkin' coma for about three weeks, porin' over tide charts, studyin' Indian legends, and makin' all kinds of astrological calculations. It was all Greek to me, but three moons later he had me out dancin' on the mudflats again, and sweet Jesus if we didn't catch another one!*

SQI: Just how big was the creature?

Cleats: *About the size of a cantaloupe, as I recall. Felt like an old, overripe one, too. Back then there was so many of 'em they were a whole lot smaller than they are nowadays. Anyway, we dumped it in the machine, and by damn if we didn't end up with <u>another</u> piece of fine pigskin.*

SQI: So, from this, ah, humble beginning the powerful squim industry was born?

Cleats: *That was Victoria's doin', some years later. Selig never got no farther than turnin' the squimskin into belts, wallets, and such. The workmanship was crappy, but he made a success of it 'cause of the gold rush of '97. There was quite a shortage of leather products, you know, and folks with gold fever was lookin' for durable goods, not fancy ones. And if squimskin's anything, it's durable. Hell, I hear tell some of that leather's been reworked, and is still around today . . . .*

SL: How did he meet the demand?

Cleats: *He rehired them assistants of his . . . you know, the ones that'd helped him with his face-liftin' machine . . . . Problem was, they was still bitter from bein' booted out of their cushy jobs in the first place, and they was just waitin' for a chance to stab him in the back. After they learned his secret, they tried settin' up their own business. All hell broke loose when Selig found out, let me tell you . . . . That was a bad time, that was . . . sparked off the grim Squim War of '99. That was sure one sorry affair. When they finally realized they couldn't beat him, they poisoned the flats and damn near killed off all the squim . . . .*

SL: Could you tell us more about Victoria? You implied she was the one who was actually responsible for the industry's success.

Cleats: Oh, yes. Miz Vickie . . . Selig called her "Schultzie". Her husband, Ruston, is from the Dutch side of the Schultz family. Anyhow, she reconciled with her father in '23 . . . would've been . . . let's see . . . about 18 or 19 at the time, I reckon. Anyway, she took a good hard look at Selig's business, recognized the unusual quality of the leather, and smelled a fortune. Next thing you know Ruston had come out from Brooklyn, and the three of 'em worked out a deal. Ruston knew where the money was, that's for sure . . . . He took some sample squimskin and went back east, then to some Mediterranean island. A few months later he turns back up and begins sloshin' money around like it was vino, settin' up a big factory and distribution center on the north end of Tacoma. We was all sworn to secrecy about the squim and the factory. Everybody was pretty much agreed that nobody in their right mind would buy the "pigskin" if they realized it was made out of somethin' that looks like the dumpins of a spittoon a year after the spittin's over.

SQI: Did you work for the company from the very beginning?

Cleats: Nope. Tried my hand at loggin', fishin', dancin', and freelance thumpin' around the Sound for a few years first. But then, in '32, they made me an offer I couldn't refuse — Master Thumper at the main factory in Tacoma . . . it was camouflaged as a kind of copper smelter. Pretty clever, being as how both factories smell pretty much the same . . . .

SQI: Could you tell . . . .

Cleats: Oh! Hold on a second. I gotta tell you a lucrative sideline I had goin' up till I retired: scrapin' little bits of arsenic out of the factory smokestacks, sprinklin' it on chocolates, and then sellin' 'em at the Market in

Seatty. Lots of girls used to eat it to look pale-like, you know. Business slumped for a while, but it picked back up when the punk look came in . . . .

SQI: What else do you remember about the family?

Cleats: Well, Ruston was sure one shrewd businessman, that's for sure. Everything was goin' along just fine, what with the wars and all, until . . . until . . . [begins to sob] *. . . the EPA* . . . .

SQI: Are you all right, Mr. Yaeger? Here, let me get you a glass of water . . . .

Cleats: [recovering] *No, no, I'm all right. Well, thank God for the Squim Institute, that's all I can say. With the factory shot, who's goin' to take care of the little ones . . . all that thumpin' in vain* . . . .

SQI: You haven't yet said anything about Wakefield's son, Mortimer.

Cleats: Well, it's funny how things turned out. It was in '32, the same year I got the job as Master Thumper, that Mort comes home after livin' in Paris for a number of years. He was the most political man I ever met. Real passionate guy, he was, always lookin' for some kind of wrong to right, 'specially anything he thought smacked of cruelty to animals. He was a nice enough guy, I guess, but just not practical. So Ruston, he told Selig that Mort was causin' mischief for the business, and to find him something to do to keep him out of trouble — or else. So Selig got the bright idea of cre- atin' the Squim Institute and puttin' Mort in charge of studyin' how to develop squim waste products into an industrial fertilizer or somethin' . . . he wasn't allowed at the factory, so I rarely saw him. They set it up in Sequim, Washington, on the Olympic Peninsula — havin'

*it there was a sort of cover for the operation, I reckon.
That's about all I know about Mort, 'cept that he kept
careful research records, thank the Lord.*

SQI: *You were close to Schultzie and Ruston?*

Cleats: *Close as you can get. Schultzie's death in '49
hurt us deep. Last I heard of Ruston, he'd been called
overseas to meet with the board . . . .*

SQI: Thank you, sir, for . . . .

Cleats: *'Scuse me, but I'd just like to say it feels good
to spill the beans after keepin' this whole business secret for so long. I'm glad to help out any way I can. I
gotta admit there's a soft spot in my heart for the little
critters after bein' around 'em so long . . . . Oh, and
I do love thumpin' and such . . . . Oh, and be sure to
tell your readers to try out my recipes — they're real
good. And remember to thump for fun . . . and good
squimming!*

REFERENCES

Published Works:

Editorial: "The Ugliest Things," *Picayune Times* New Orleans, April 6, 1897, p. 3.

Lawrence M. Dill, Ph.D., "Behavioral Genetics of the Sidehill Gouger," *The Journal of Irreproducible Results,* New York: Workman Publishing, 1983, pp. 9-10.

Indiana Jones, *Memoirs,* Boston: Anthropologicial Society Press, 1947.

S. Lee, *Sumo Wrestling Handbook,* Tokyo: Fujiyama Publications, 1956.

Leonardo Da Vinci *Notebooks,* 112E-C.

T. Moonchild, *The Sex Magick of Aleister Crowley,* London: Golden Dawn Press, 1931.

T. Rex, *Dinosaur Diets: Fads and Fallacies.* Shanghai: Anglo-Sino Publishing, 1927, pp. 131-33.

M. "Cleats" Yaeger, *The Compleat Mudsteader: Use Ooze to Build Your Dream House,* Sequim: The SQI Publications, 1974.

Unpublished Works:

Collette St. Germain, *The Eggs and I,* SQI Research Reports. Research conducted as interim director at SQI from M. Wakefield's death to appointment of new director. Vol. XXX, pp. 733-738, 1980.

Mortimer H. Wakefield, Ph.D., *Collected Verse,* MSS in Squim Institute Library, Sequim, Washington, 1944.

Works in Progress:

B. Wakefield-Dunn, ed., *The Squim Encyclopedia.* To be published in 30 volumes. In press at SQI Publications, 1986.

M. "Cleats" Yaeger, *Dancin' in the Dark.* A series of interviews with SQI, to be published in 24 volumes. In press at SQI Publications, 1986.

Other:

Lower Sloane Launderers, London, ticket number 71-71 for "one ornate codpiece," signed by "Al Crowley, Esq."

LAST "GASP" PROGRAM

If you are unable to pledge, you can still help save the squim from extinction. As Jacques Cousteau would say, in our situation, "Viva la flatulation." Help out by becoming a member of "Guardian Auxiliary for Squim Preservation" (GASP). Membership categories are:

Larva **$2.95**
Membership benefits include:
(1) Official SQI "Save the Squim" membership card
(2) "Save the Squim" button

Yearling **$5.95**
Same benefits as "Larvae," plus:
"Save the Squim" bumper sticker

Adult **$13.95**
Same benefits as "Yearling," plus:
"Monarch of the Mudflat" t-shirt

"Behemoth" **$23,095**
Same benefits as "Adult," plus:
Quit-claim deed to an abandoned squimmery

To become a member, write SQI at the address below and indicate the category of membership. "Save the Squim" promotional products may be ordered separately. Button price is $1.95. Bumper sticker price is $2.95. T-shirt price is $8.95. When ordering t-shirts, please specify size (S, M, L, XL).

> To become a member, or to place an order for a "Save the Squim" product, write:
> THE SQUIM INSTITUTE
> P.O. Box 4711
> Rolling Bay, WA 98061